STAR WARS®

phoenix international publications, inc.

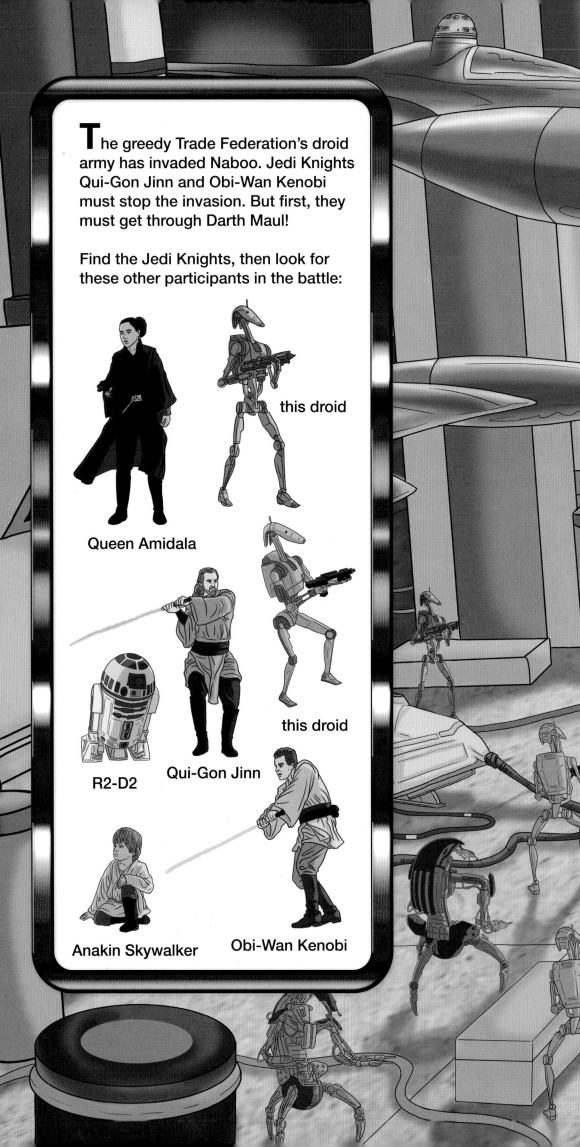

The greedy Trade Federation's droid army has invaded Naboo. Jedi Knights Qui-Gon Jinn and Obi-Wan Kenobi must stop the invasion. But first, they must get through Darth Maul!

Find the Jedi Knights, then look for these other participants in the battle:

Queen Amidala

this droid

R2-D2

Qui-Gon Jinn

this droid

Anakin Skywalker

Obi-Wan Kenobi

Senator Amidala has been attacked! The brave Jedi Knights Anakin Skywalker and Obi-Wan Kenobi chase the Senator's attacker into a seedy nightclub on Coruscant.

Search the scene for the attacker and these other nightclub guests:

Anakin Skywalker

this dancer

this waitress

this customer

Obi-Wan Kenobi

Zam Wesell

When Obi-Wan visits Kamino, he discovers that a massive army of clones is being built for the Republic. Obi-Wan has a bad feeling about this!

Not all clones are exactly alike. Search the scene for these clone commanders:

The evil Sith Lord Darth Sidious has taken control of the Republic and declared himself Emperor! Can Master Yoda put an end to this evil reign?

While Yoda battles the Emperor, search for these platforms that get in their way:

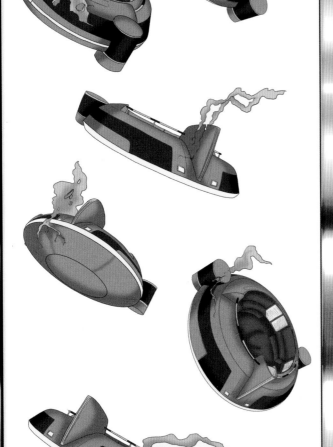

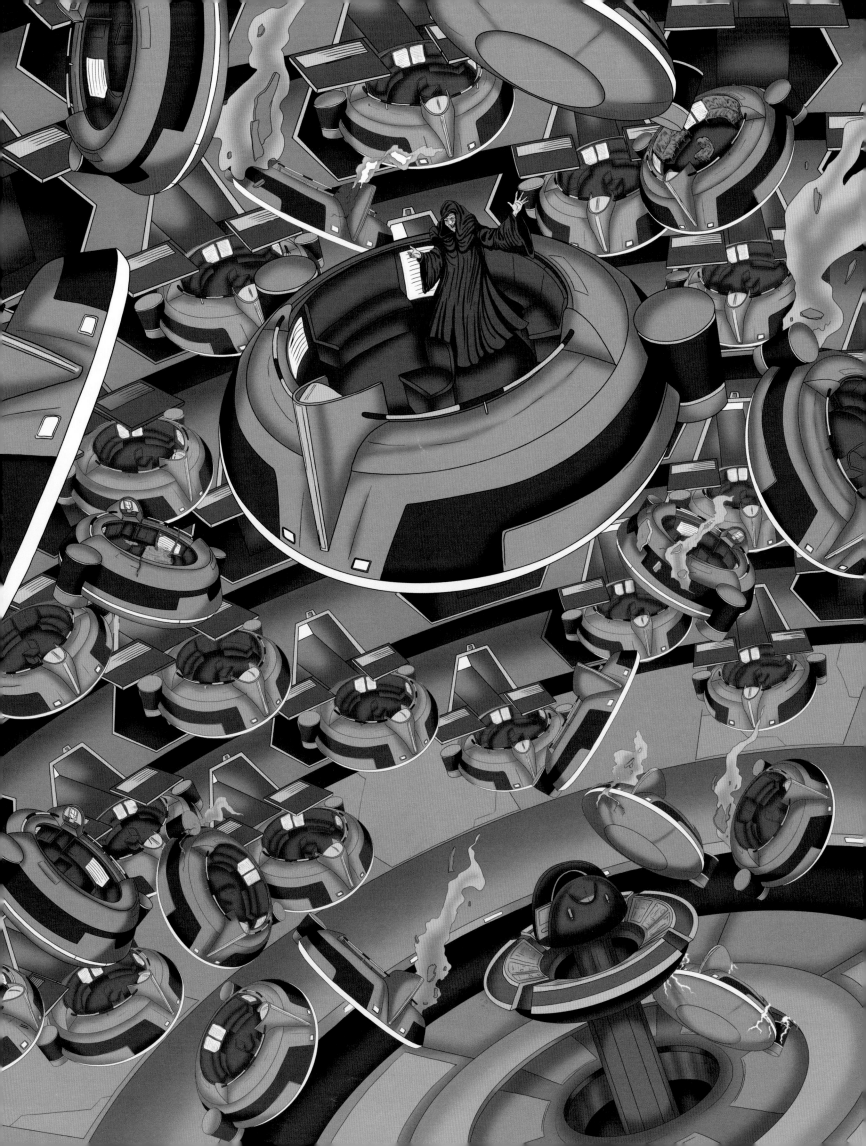

Darth Vader has captured the brave rebel leader Princess Leia. Luke Skywalker, Han Solo, and Obi-Wan Kenobi enter the Death Star on a rescue mission! Getting in was easy. Getting out is the hard part!

Help the heroes avoid these villains as they race for the *Millennium Falcon*:

Grand Moff Tarkin   Admiral Motti

this stormtrooper   this Imperial officer

Darth Vader

this stormtrooper

After the destruction of the Death Star, the evil Darth Vader attacks the rebel base on the icy planet Hoth.

While Vader looks for the rebels, see what else you can find in the cold:

Luke Skywalker

this AT-AT

this snowspeeder

this AT-AT

dish turret

this tauntaun

Luke Skywalker leaves the rebels and travels to the Dagobah system. Here, he'll complete his Jedi training with the mysterious and powerful Jedi Master Yoda.

While Luke concentrates on his training, concentrate on the scene and search for R2-D2, Yoda, and these items:

R2-D2

Luke's lunch

Yoda

this crate

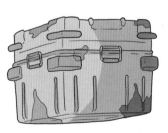

this crate

Luke's lightsaber

Luke Skywalker and the rebels have defeated the evil Emperor Palpatine and restored peace to the galaxy! Now, it's time to party!

While the rebels celebrate, look for these party guests:

Princess Leia

Anakin Skywalker

Obi-Wan Kenobi

Chewbacca

C-3PO

R2-D2

Luke Skywalker

Han Solo

Fly back to the hangar on Naboo and help the heroes spot these extra-dangerous droidekas:

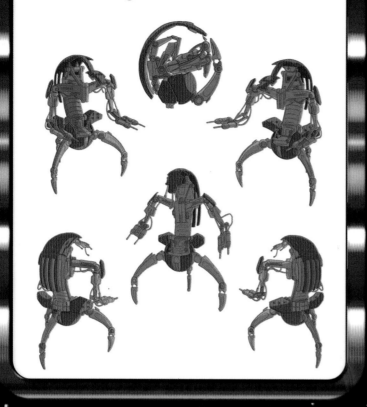

Are you ready for some droidball? Head back to the Coruscant nightclub and search for these big fans:

Go back to Kamino and find **10** clone helmets hidden around the clone factory.

Return to the Galactic Senate and search for the platforms belonging to these planets:

Kamino

Rodia

Naboo

Kashyyyk

Alderaan

"Blast the door, kid!" Return to the Death Star and help the heroes find these control switches so they can escape:

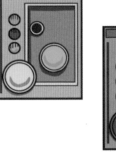

Brrrr! Bundle up and head back to the Battle of Hoth to look for these droids, Hoth dwellers, and other very cold things:

R2-D2

wampa

snowman
rebel trooper

frozen snowspeeder

frozen probe droid

Dagobah seems quiet, but it's teeming with life. Return to Yoda's planet and search for these strange creatures:

this nudj

this sleen

this bogwing

this bogwing

swamp slug

this pikobi

The party isn't over! Head back to the celebration to find these Ewoks who love to have a good time: